# THE CTS COMPANION TO PRAYING WITH THE BIBLE

by
Fr Z Mattam S.D.B.

*All booklets are published thanks to the
generous support of the members of the
Catholic Truth Society*

## CATHOLIC TRUTH SOCIETY
PUBLISHERS TO THE HOLY SEE

# CONTENTS

**Acknowledgments**

This booklet, reproduced here by kind permission of Kristu Jyoti
Publications, was first published in 1998 as part of a larger work,
'Opening the Bible'.

## THE NATURE OF PRAYER

*Luke 18:9-14*

Before speaking about ways of praying with the Bible we must investigate a little about the nature of prayer. What does real prayer consist of? What are its conditions? There are some attitudes and dispositions which are essential to be able to enter into dialogue with God, in prayer.

### The problem of prayer

Prayer is an art which no one gains mastery of all of a sudden. Everyone has to struggle their way through, and in the process one often feels like giving up. So often our prayer instead of being what it is meant to be, an encounter, a meeting between God and us, seems to become a monologue, there is no encounter, no meeting. It is like trying to speak to someone on the phone with no one seeming to listen and respond on the other end of the line. After some time, one invariably feels like giving up and going away. What's wrong? How does one establish this contact with God in Prayer? What are the attitudes and dispositions which are basic to any prayer experience? In His parable of the Pharisee and the tax collector Jesus Christ gives us a lesson on prayer. Let us examine it.

### The Pharisee speaks to himself

Jesus presents to us two people at prayer. The prayer of one of these, that of the Pharisee, ends up by being a monologue: there is no encounter, no meeting. The text says: 'the Pharisee stood and prayed thus to himself' (*18:11*). He was not praying to God; he was speaking to himself. There really was no one at the other end of the line! His prayer was a waste of time. Perhaps he was communing with his inner self but certainly he was not reaching any higher. He was not reaching God, and our Lord makes this point clear.

The prayer of the tax collector, was instead a genuine dialogue with God; there is an encounter, a meeting. He goes home having been justified, touched by God, reconciled with Him, in communion with Him.

But why was there no meeting, no encounter when the Pharisee prayed? And what was it that made this meeting and encounter possible when the publican prayed?

### Who were the Pharisees?

First of all it will help to recall who the Pharisees and Publicans were. The derivation of the name Pharisee probably comes from the Hebrew *'parash'* meaning, "one who is separate" or "holy one." They separated themselves from the mass of people who took to liberal Greek ways of living and they applied themselves to the perfect observance of the law. In their zeal for the law they went beyond what the law required. If the law commanded that every Israelite should fast once a year, they would fast twice a week. They would count even the small garden herbs and plants like mint and dill and cumin (*Mt. 23:23*) and pay tithes on them. They would give alms generously, and would never miss the prescribed times of prayer, even if they were at that time in the streets or in the market place.

## Who were the tax collectors?

The tax collectors on the other hand, were Jewish underlings employed by Roman officialdom in Palestine to do the actual collecting of tolls from those transporting property (including slaves) by land or sea. The Romans gave this right to collect taxes for a stipulated sum to private contractors, who in their turn tried to amass wealth. Thus we read that Zacchaeus who was the chief of the tax collectors had through his job become very rich (*Lk. 19:2-10*). These men were regarded as doubly base and despicable. They were people who had sold their services to a foreign oppressor, the Romans, and they were most often extortionists themselves engaging in real robbery. The rabbis equated them with robbers and held that they and their family were barred from holding communal office and even from giving testimony in a Jewish court, or taking part in communal worship. The Gospels repeatedly put tax collectors with sinners. (*Mt. 9:10-11; 11:19; Mk.*

*2:15-16; Lk. 5:30*) and sometimes with prostitutes (*Mt. 21:31*) and gentiles (*Mt. 18:17*).

## The tax collector spoke from the heart

Why was the prayer of such a man heard? What is it that made a meeting, an encounter with God possible when such a man prayed? The publican was aware of his true reality. He was living in the truth. He did not approach God with a mask. This was a prayer that came from the heart. He was aware of the hopelessness of his case. He had really defrauded and extorted. He was really a sinner and he did not try to hide it or excuse himself. "Would not even lift up his eyes to heaven, but beat his breast saying, God, be merciful to me a sinner" (*Lk. 18:13*). God cannot resist the prayer of a contrite and broken heart and looking down upon him forgave him and justified him.

## The Pharisee was estranged from the truth about himself

The Pharisee instead was alienated from his true reality. His prayer came only from his lips. He was putting forward some one who was not his real self. His external behaviour and good works, which were more a product of his social status and upbringing, had blinded him to the fact that he was a loveless person, self-centred and egoistic, self-righteous and proud, filled with contempt and scorn for others, "the rest of men". It was true he fasted, prayed and gave tithes of all his possessions but all this was done to win the admiration of men, to be seen by them. In reality he was using religion to build himself up and did not have any genuine love for God. He refused to accept this truth about himself and therefore God could not enter into dialogue with him. However, God could enter into dialogue with the tax collector because he knew fully well his true reality and accepted it before God.

## Christian prayer: meeting God in one's existential situation

This may also be the reason why often we fail to make contact with God in prayer. Like the Pharisee we may be putting forward someone who is not our real self. We are often estranged from our true reality and live quite detached from ourselves. We live so superficially, so immersed in what is happening around us, so filled with constant offerings of the mass media, that we hardly have time to enter into the depth of our being where God waits for us.

Christian prayer is not some kind of nirvana or escape from our reality, it is to meet Christ in our existential situation; in the depth of our reality. The first task of the Word of God is to illuminate our lives and show us who we really are. Christian prayer is a shout for help raised to God from the depth of the reality of our helplessness and need.

It is symbolic that we cannot see our own face. We cannot see what we look like. We recognise persons by their faces; it is the face that gives the identity to a person but we cannot see our own face. We need a mirror to see what we look like, to know our identity. To know who we are we must look into a mirror. But what determines our true identity, the person we really are is not our face, but our heart. And we do not know what is in our heart. God has given us a mirror for this: It is the Word of God. It 'pierces like a two edged sword' to the division of soul and spirit, of joints and marrow, revealing the thoughts and intentions of the heart (*Heb. 4:12*). To pray we need to enter into our heart.

### The meeting with God takes place in the heart

The heart is something that lies deep within us. In the Biblical sense the heart stands for the inner core of our being, the root of our existence. To pray one must pass beyond the senses, feelings, sentiments, imagination and reason, to the heart or the spirit of man. It is there that the encounter with God takes place. As St Paul says: "It is the Spirit Himself bearing witness with our spirit that we are children of God" (*Rom. 8:16*). There, in the spirit of man the meeting between God and man takes place. It is from this central point of our being, the ontological centre of our person that we address God in prayer. "For out of abundance of the heart his mouth speaks" (*Lk. 6:45*). Prayer is a heart that overflows with joy, contrition, gratitude and praise.

### The Pharisee estranged from God

The first reason why the Pharisee's prayer was not heard was that he was alienated from his true self. But the Pharisee was not only alienated from himself, he was also alienated from God. He had an idea of God which was far from true. He regarded God as a kind of task master, a law giver, concerned only with the law and its fulfilment. His idea of God was of one who had nothing to do with sinners, with those who are "extortioners, unjust, adulterous like the rest of mankind" (*Lk. 18:11*). But this is not the God who revealed himself to us in the Scriptures. Such a God did not exist. It was only the figment of his imagination, and therefore, naturally his prayer had to end in a monologue. There really was no one on the other end of the line.

The tax collector instead knew fully well that God was above all a Father who loved his children even when they had fallen into sins. He knew that his sins far from repelling God only drew Him all the more close to him, because he was so much in need of His mercy and help. In other words he knew that God loved him as he was and accepted him as he was. St Teresa defined prayer as "a conversation with the one who we know loves us". No conversation is possible unless there is this awareness of being loved, of being forgiven, of being accepted as we are. God cannot really enter into dialogue with us as long as we doubt His love and forgiveness. "In this is love, not that we loved God, but that he loved us and sent his Son to be the expiation of our sins" (*1 Jn. 4:10*).

Therefore, if we wish to meet God in prayer we must cast off a great many misguided notions and go to the God who manifested Himself to us in the Scriptures: God, the Father of our Lord Jesus Christ who revealed himself on the cross as total love, as total mercy, as total forgiveness, even for those who killed His Son. Pray then like this, says Jesus, "Our father who art in heaven" (*Mt. 6:9*). Prayer is conversation with our Father and not rendering account to a heartless law giver or judge.

### The Pharisee estranged from his neighbour

Thirdly, the Pharisee was not only estranged from himself and from God, but also from his fellow men. He separates himself from the rest of mankind and especially from the tax collector whom he judges and despises. "I thank thee God that I am not like other men, extortioners, unjust, adulterers or even grasping, like this tax collector' (*Lk. 18:11*). We can never approach God in isolation, separating ourselves from other brothers and sisters and especially from those closest to us. To be reconciled with them, to be in communion with them is a basic condition for any prayer. "If you are offering your gift at the altar and there remember that your brother has something against you, leave your gift there before the altar and go; first be reconciled to your brother, and then come and offer your gift" (*Mt. 5:23-25*). Again more explicitly in Mk. 11:25: "And whenever you stand praying, forgive, if you have anything against any one; so that your Father also who is in heaven may forgive you your trespasses."

## Christ brings us to the Father

Jesus Christ said: "Whatever you ask in my name, I will do it, that the Father may be glorified in the Son. If you ask anything in my name, I will do it". (*Jn. 14:13-14*). Again in John 16:23-24: "Truly, truly I say to you, if you ask anything of the Father, he will give it to you in my name. Hitherto you have asked for nothing in my name; ask, and you will receive, that your joy may be full". The name according to the Bible is inseparable from the person and shares his prerogatives. To pray in the name of Jesus means to pray in communion and fellowship with Him. Thus in John 15:7 we read, "If you abide in me, and my words abide in you, ask whatever you will and it shall be done for you". Jesus Christ is total communion with God and with man. When man had through his sins been cut off from God and been unable to reach Him again, Jesus Christ became man and united Himself totally with him, identifying Himself with us and standing before the Father as the guilty one, bearing our sins, and suffering the punishment we deserved. In Christ and through Christ we sinners can have access to the Father, because after His resurrection He poured forth His spirit into our hearts by which we can cry 'Abba', Father (*Rom. 8:15*). "Likewise the Spirit helps us in our weakness; for we do not know how to pray as we ought, but the Spirit himself intercedes for us with sighs too deep for words" (*Rom. 8:26*). We learn to pray when we can attune ourselves and make our own this intercession of the Spirit in our hearts. The Holy Spirit is the real master and guide given us by Christ to lead us to the depths of prayer.

## Conclusion

From this lesson of Christ on prayer we can understand its nature and conditions. Prayer is a conversation with the Father who loves us and accepts us as we are. But this dialogue with God takes place in our existential situation and therefore the first condition for prayer is the awareness of one's sinfulness and need, and the second is that of being in communion with others, forgiving from the heart any injury or hurt received. We must therefore begin our prayer by bringing to mind our sins and asking pardon for them and, secondly, by recalling the persons who may have hurt us and forgiving them from the heart and praying for them. Thirdly, we can go to the Father only in the name of, and in communion and fellowship with, Christ.

## PRAYING THE PSALMS

The Bible has within it a prayer book, and it is the Book of the Psalter (the Psalms). In it we have the divinely inspired response to the self-revelation of God. When the people of Israel experienced the overwhelming love of God in being chosen among all the peoples of the world to be God's own special Possession, and in being privileged to receive His self-revelation, living presence and covenant, they did not know how to respond to Him. Therefore, God Himself inspired this response and so to say put on their lips the words with which they could speak to Him, thank Him and praise Him. This is the Psalter. The Psalms are the expression of an experience of God. They are songs of men who knew who God was. In them they are singing of their knowledge of God and of their union with Him.

### Prayer book of the Church

The Church puts this book in the hands of her priests, religious men and women and even lay people because the Psalms in reality speak of her relationship to God. The mystery of God's self-revelation and self-gift to Israel in the Old Testament was only the figure of what was to be accomplished in Christ and in the Church. God has given Himself totally to man in Christ. God's union with His people in the Old Testament looks forward to Christ's union with the Church. God's self-revelation to the people of Israel through the Covenant at Sinai looks forward to His self-gift to us in Jesus Christ in the New Covenant. In singing the Psalms which speak of God's love for Israel, the Church is therefore singing of her union with Jesus Christ. The Church calls the Psalms her "Wedding Hymn". They are the expression of her deepest inner life. They spring from her innermost heart. They express her soul, her desires, her sorrows, her joys. *The Constitution on Sacred Liturgy (SC)* calls it the voice of the Bride addressing the Bridegroom (*SC. No. 84*).

## Psalms fulfilled in Jesus Christ

The fathers of the Church said that the book of the Psalter was a closed book, sealed with seven seals; the image is found in The Book of the Apocalypse 5:1. But the Apocalypse also speaks of one who held the key of David (*Rev. 3:7*). This person whom the Apocalypse identifies as Christ is the one who can break the seven seals and make the Psalter an open book. In Lk. 24:44 Jesus himself clearly affirms this truth when he says: "Everything written about me in the law of Moses and the Prophets and the Psalms must be fulfilled". Jesus Christ has fulfilled the Psalms in Himself. Hence when today we pray the Psalms, we are praying them as given to us fulfilled in Jesus Christ. Jesus Christ gives a new significance to the Psalms.

The whole Bible has only one single content: The mystery of Christ. From the very beginning, salvation history was made for and compressed towards the mystery of Christ. Jesus says, "Your father Abraham rejoiced that he was to see my day; he saw it and was glad" (*Jn. 8:56*). Abraham and the Patriarchs were already living the mystery of Christ in an incipient way. And the Psalms in which we find an echo of these earlier experiences speak to us about the living mystery of Christ, though often in a vague and obscure way.

## A re-reading required to pray the Psalms

When the Church prays the Psalms today, she does not pray them as Israel of the Old Testament did. She prays them as fulfilled in Jesus Christ. For this, a re-reading is required. In fact we know that such a process of re-reading was already done in the Old Testament. Thus, after the exile and again at the time of the writing of the Greek Septuagint many Psalms which originally spoke of the kingship, of suffering etc. were understood messianically.

The Royal Psalms were interpreted as speaking of the kingship of the Messiah. David himself was thought of more and more as the figure of the Messiah. This is why the Book of Chronicles presents him as an ideal figure with no faults. For this reason also all the Davidic Psalms were interpreted messianically. The Psalms of suffering were considered as speaking of the sufferings of the

Messiah, and the Psalms of supplication as expressing the anguish of the Messiah and already as an anticipation of his suffering on the Cross. The Psalms of enthronement were applied to the enthronement of the Messiah and the inauguration of the messianic kingdom.

The New Testament continues and perfects this re-reading of the Psalter. It is enough to look at the way Peter and Paul use Ps. 110, 16, 2 in their sermons (*Acts Chapters 2, 13 etc.*). And the Epistle to the Hebrews quotes the verses from Ps. 2, 8, 45, 97, 102, 103, 110, etc. as words spoken by the Father to the Son.

Jesus Christ is therefore the full and real meaning of the Psalms and what they express is the mystery of Christ, His Passion, Death and Resurrection and the mystery of the Church He was to found. It is in this sense that we must pray them today.

## Psalms of repentance

What about the Psalms of repentance which confess sins? How can they be referred to Christ? The Fathers of the Church said that in these Psalms Christ was speaking in our name. Having identified himself with man, he stood before the Father bearing all our sins and interceding with the Father in our name. On the cross Christ really bore our sins; today when we pray them we know that because Jesus Christ took our place and bore the consequences of our sins and therefore we can have access to the Father.

## Psalms containing malediction

What about the Psalms of malediction? Can they be referred to Christ? And again, can we pray them today? We need to do a re-reading of these Psalms to be able to use them in prayer. First of all we have to realise that these imprecations were uttered against the enemies of the people of Israel, against the powers that tried to destroy the people belonging to God. Now what destroys God's work in us is Satan and our own sins. We can truly pray them with Christ wishing for the final and total destruction of Satan and all evil in the world. Again, Jesus Christ died on the cross praying for his enemies. Taking the place of sinners He took on Himself all the curses that we sinners deserved. "He became a curse for us" (*Gal. 3:13*) says St Paul. This also is the only attitude a Christian can have before his enemies. We can therefore pray these Psalms as words directed against the powers of evil, or aware that through our sins we were these enemies against whom these imprecations were said. And knowing that Jesus took our place when we were His enemies, we can pray that God give us also the same attitude of love and forgiveness towards our enemies.

## Life transformed into prayer

The Psalms can teach us to transform our lives into a prayer. The material of the Psalms is essentially human and the natural experiences of joy, sorrow, failure, sickness, sin, fear, anguish, pain, desperation, expectation, etc. But these are lived by the Psalmist with God. The Psalmist transforms them into prayer. Praying the Psalms in these situations, we too are led to transform these situations into prayer. To give an example: according to tradition David after his sin composed the Ps. 51: "Have mercy on me God according to thy steadfast love; according to thy abundant mercy and a blot out my transgressions" (*Ps. 51:1*). Today a person who has fallen into the same or a similar sin can use this Psalm to meet God. Similarly the other Psalms, can teach us how to transform experiences of suffering and failure, joy and sorrow, sickness and leisure into prayer and lead us to encounter God in them. By praying the Psalms Christians will grow to more mature prayer life, becoming assimilated into the attitude of Christ towards His Father.

## Prayer of Christ and of the Church

When we pray the Psalms today we are not praying them in our name but that of Christ. The Psalter is the vicarious prayer of Christ for His Church. When we pray the Psalms we speak to the Father in the person His Divine Son, moved by the Spirit. This prayer belongs not to the individual member, but to the whole Body of Christ. Only in the whole Christ, does the whole Psalter become a reality. Very often some verses of the Psalms may not express our reality, but they are nevertheless true of some other members of the Body of Christ, and when we pray them we are praying them in their name. In the *General*

*Instruction to the Breviary,* No. 13, we read: "Christ is present when His community comes together, when the word of God is proclaimed and when the Church prays and sings". The Christian will be helped to see his prayer as a sharing in the prayer of Christ, to deepen his faith in his oneness with Christ through the Holy Spirit, and to be aware when he prays, of "our voice in Him and His voice in us" as St Augustine said.

## Conclusion

The Psalms stem from an experience of God and can lead us to an experience of God. They can form in us the mind of Christ and help us to develop an interior life which is truly biblical and ecclesial. They not only direct our thoughts and affections to God, but they establish us in God and unite us to him, because the sentiments and thoughts of the Psalmist are sentiments and thoughts of God. They teach us to praise Him on all occasions, in sorrow as well as joy and enable us to begin on earth our eternal life of praise.

## THE OUR FATHER:
## THE PATTERN OF CHRISTIAN PRAYER

If prayer is a conversation with the Father, what will the child of God speak to Him about? What is the format and content of this dialogue? This is given in the Our Father.

### The pattern and school of Christian Prayer

When the disciples ask Jesus, "Lord teach us to pray, as John taught his disciples" (*Lk. 11:1*), He told them, "When you pray, say..." (*Lk. 11:2*), and went on to teach the Our Father. This therefore is how a disciple must pray. The Our Father is the pattern of all Christian Prayer. A Christian's prayer has a particular format and content. There are certain things he must pray about and pray for.

The prayer of a disciple of Christ is radically different from that of a religious pagan, who goes to the temple with a gift for the deity hoping to win some favour from him. Most often this form of prayer consists in asking God for help to escape from one's problems. God becomes a kind of problem solver. As soon as there is a problem, a need, a sickness or a suffering the devout pagan runs to the temple asking God to intervene and take him out of it. Christian prayer differs from this radically. A true Christian, prays always and only that God's will be done in his life, because he knows that whatever

God wills is the best for him. In the Gospel Jesus Christ says: "And in praying do not heap up empty phrases as the Gentiles do; for they think that they will be heard for their many words. Do not be like them, for your Father knows what you need before you ask him". (*Mt. 6:7-.8*) Then He goes on to teach the Our Father.

## A prayer only Christians can pray

The Our Father then is the typical Christian prayer. At the time of Jesus, every religious sect had its own specific prayer. The disciples of John had prayers taught by John. The disciples of the Pharisees likewise had their prayers. The Our Father is the prayer of Christ's disciples. More over, it is a prayer which only a disciple can pray, because only on his lips has it full meaning.

In the early Church, the Our Father was kept secret from the Catechumen until the appropriate moment of the Christian initiation either just before baptism or, in some places like Jerusalem, immediately after it. And it was only after having received this Sacrament that he was allowed to recite it with the other believers. The Prayer presupposes that the one who prays it has heard the Good News of the Gospel, and having believed it, has undergone a conversion of heart and receiving Baptism and forgiveness of sins has become in this way a child of God. In Baptism one is really born of the Father, and so can in all truth call him Father. On the lips of those who did not have this experience, the words of this prayer would be meaningless.

## Our Father who art in heaven

While Matthew has the long form of address, 'Our Father who art in heaven', Luke has only the short expression, 'Father'. Studies carried out by Joachim Jeremias and others, show that Jesus Christ habitually addressed the Father with the term 'Abba'. Mark has preserved for us the prayer of Jesus in Gethsemane, "Abba, Father, all things are possible to thee; remove this cup from me; yet not what I will, but what thou wilt" (*Mk. 14:36*). Abba is the diminutive vocative taken from the language of children, similar to our 'Daddy'. The word expressed trust, familiarity, tenderness. The rabbis could never think of using this word to address God in prayer. It would have been the expression of total disrespect for God according to them. (Joachim Jeremias, *The Lord's Prayer*, (Philadelphia, 1964)

### Expression of a unique sonship

The term Abba used by Christ to address the Father, is the expression of a unique filiation. The early Church spoke of God as "the Father of Our Lord Jesus Christ" (*Rom. 15:6*). We see how in the Gospels Jesus Christ is always conscious of a unique relationship between Him and the Father. We see it already at the age of twelve in his reply to his mother and foster-father after the loss and finding in the temple: "How is it that you sought me? Did you not know that I must be in my Father's house?" (*Lk. 2:49*). But it is especially St John's Gospel that brings out this intimate union of Christ with the Father vividly. He is the only begotten Son of the Father (*1:14*) who is in the bosom of the Father (*1:18*). The Father loves the Son and has given all things into his hands (*3:35*). "Truly, truly, I say to you, the Son can do nothing of His own accord, but only what He sees the Father doing; for whatever He does, that the Son does likewise. For the Father loves the Son, and shows Him all that He himself is doing (*5:19-20*). Philip said to him, "Lord, show us the Father and we shall be satisfied"; Jesus said to him, "Have I been with you so long, and yet you do not know me, Philip? He who has seen me has seen the Father; how can you say, show us the Father? Do you not believe that I am in the Father and the Father in me? The words I say to you, I do not speak on my own authority but the Father who dwells in me does his works. Believe me that I am in the Father and the Father in me; or else believe me for the sake of the works themselves". (*Jn. 14:8-11*)

In John the term Son *(huios)* is reserved for Jesus and the term child *(teknon)* for the disciple. He is the only begotten Son in the real sense of the word: the well beloved Son (*Mk. 12:6*). Never does Jesus at any time address God "Our Father', as though God could be in the same way His Father and the Father of the disciples. "Go to my brethren and say to them, I am ascending to my Father, and to your Father, to my God and to your God" (*Jn. 20:17*).

## The divine sonship of Christians

If the disciples were astonished and even shocked a little by Jesus' use of the term Abba for God, we can imagine how much more wonderstruck and astonished they would have been at the fact that the Christians can also address God in the same way. As the words of the liturgy says, it would have been only at the express command of the Lord that they would have dared to call him, Abba, Father. "When the time had fully come, God sent forth his Son, born of woman, born under the law, to redeem those who were under the law, so that we might receive adoption as sons. And because you are sons, God sent the Spirit of his Son, into your hearts crying 'Abba, Father'. So through God you are no longer a slave, but a son, and if a son then an heir" (*Gal. 4:4-7*). "For you did not receive the spirit of slavery to fall back into fear, but you have received the spirit of sonship. When we cry, "Abba Father!", it is the Spirit himself bearing witness with our spirit that we are children of God, and if children, then heirs, heirs of God and fellow heirs with Christ, provided we suffer with him in order that we may also be glorified with him" (*Rom. 8:15-18*). The divine filiation of

Christians is no *metaphorical thing*, because at Baptism they are really made to share in the life of God himself. "To all who received him, who believed in his name, he gave the power to become children of God; who were born not of blood, nor of the will of the flesh, nor of the will of man, but of God himself" (*Jn. 1:12-13*) "See what love the Father has given us that we should be called children of God; and so we are. The reason why the world does not know us is that it did not know him. Beloved we are God's children now; it does not yet appear what we shall be, but we know that when he appears we shall be like him, for we shall see him as he is" (*1 Jn. 3:1-2*).

## In heaven

The phrase 'in heaven' acts as a kind of caution against the danger of too much familiarity. Even though we can address Him 'Abba', we must never forget that he remains the all holy transcendent God.

## Hallowed be thy name

In the Bible the name stands for the person. It is indicative of the future, personality and mission of the individual. When Peter for example was called *Kefa* (rock) (*Mt. 16:18*) by Jesus, it meant that henceforth he was to become the solid foundation stone of the Church. The name of God expresses His intimate and profound personality, which is ineffable and unknowable, in itself. When He revealed His

name 'Yahweh' to Moses (*Ex. 3:14*) it is not to be thought
of as the 'philosophical metaphysical definition of His
being but an existential promise to be with His people".
(Henri van Den Bussche, *Understanding the Lord's
Prayer,* New York, 1963) "The name of God is that by
which he reveals himself. Its purpose is to convey the
knowledge of who God is for those who know him, for
those upon whom his name has been invoked and who bear
his name. To know the name of Yahweh is to know what
one owes to Yahweh, and thus fundamentally to know him
as the one who supports Israel by his protective presence."

When we pray, hallowed be thy name, we are praying
that God may manifest His holiness by the revelation of
his glory and power to save man. When in John 12:28,
Jesus prays, "Father glorify thy name" this is what He
meant. On the Cross of His Son, the Father revealed His
power and glory. To save man He delivered up His Son
and raised him up for us. When we pray, hallowed by thy
name, we are praying that this power and glory be accepted by all, that all men may draw profit from them and
praise and glorify God for the wonder of His love
towards man.

## Thy kingdom come

The Kingdom of God is not the exact translation of the
*'Basilea tou theou'* in Greek, and *'Malkut d elaha'* or
*'Malkut di yy'* in Aramaic. The better translation would

be the 'reign of God' or the 'rule of God', and means not so much the domain in which Yahweh exercises His royal power as the activity through which God reveals Himself as king.

The Old Testament speaks of three different forms of Yahweh's rule. First of all Yahweh is said to be the king of Israel which He had freed from the slavery of Egypt and with whom He made a Covenant, choosing them to be His own people. After their entry into the promised land they have no kings in the beginning because it was very clear to them that Yahweh was their king; and finally when they have kings, they are considered only to be the representatives of Yahweh in whose name they rule.

Secondly, Yahweh is king of creation because he has created and sustains it. The so called Enthronement Psalms acclaim Yahweh as Creator and King (*Ps. 47, 93, 96, 97, 98*). "Who would not revere you, King of nations? Yes, this is your due. Since of all the wise among the nations, and in all their kingdoms, there is not a single one like you; He is the living God and the everlasting King. At his wrath the earth quakes, and the nations cannot endure his indignation" (*Jer. 10:7, 10*)

Thirdly, Yahweh is king in the eschatological sense, that is referring to the final and definitive coming of Yahweh's kingdom when He will establish His total and complete rule over everything, and will be acknowledged

and adored by all. All evil will be eliminated and there
will be perfect harmony in creation. (*Is. ll:lff; Mal. 1:14*)

### Jesus ushers in the Kingdom of God

The expectation and longings of the Old Testament are fulfilled in the person of Jesus who ushers in the Kingdom of
God, though not yet in glory, but nevertheless in a very
real way, which involves a break with what has gone
before, a kind of hiatus in the history of the world. "The
Kingdom of God is more than a strengthened or intensified
reign. It eliminates all that has preceded it. It 'comes' just
as the 'days come' or 'the day of Yahweh' comes *(erches-
tai)*, it arrives, or erupts *(phtanein)*; it draws near
*(eggizein)*. These terms strengthen the impression that we
are here concerned with an absolutely unique event with no
precedent whatsoever". It is present in the world in the person of Jesus (*Lk. 17:21*). The miracles He works are the
signs of the presence of the Kingdom. And in the parables
he speaks of the different aspects of the mystery of the
Kingdom. With Christ's Passion, Death and Resurrection,
the Kingdom of God comes with power, Satan's rule is
overthrown, man's sins are forgiven, and the world is reconciled with God. The Acts of the Apostles speak more of
the Holy Spirit which is poured on man, and the Gospel of
John of the new life that Jesus gives to man.

But we are still waiting for the final coming of the
Kingdom in Glory. It is for this that we are praying when

we say in the Our Father, 'Thy Kingdom come'. We are praying for the arrival of the new heaven and the new earth when God will, "Wipe away every tear from their eyes, and death shall be no more, neither shall there be mourning nor crying, nor pain anymore". (*Rev. 21:4*)

### Thy will be done on earth as it is in heaven

Tertullian said that by saying this prayer, we are exhorting ourselves to patience: *"In hoc dicto ad sufferentiam nos admonernus'.* This prayer is taken by many in the sense of a kind of resignation to the will of God which they have to accept whether they like it or not. But this is not the way the Scriptures look at the will of God. For the Bible, the will of God is man's happiness; but God can lead man to this happiness only when man allows God to fulfil His will and plan for him. All the evil in the world came about because man refused to accept the Will of God for him at the beginning of creation (*Gen. 3*). The History of Salvation starting with Abraham is an effort of God to teach man to live according to His will. Abraham accepts God's will even if it meant that he had to sacrifice his son Isaac and becomes the father of believers (*Gen. 22:15-18*). The Old Testament presents to us instances of abandonment to the will of God. Thus in 1 Sam. 3:18, Eli says to Samuel who had brought him bad news from Yahweh: 'It is the Lord; let him do what seems good to him". And Tobit who had become blind prayed, "And now deal with me according to thy pleasure; command my spirit to be taken up that I may depart and become dust' (*Tob. 3:6*). The New Testament presents to us the example of Mary who by accepting the will of God makes it possible for God to begin the work of salvation of the world, "Behold I am the handmaid of the Lord; let it be to me according to your Word" (*Lk. 1:38*). The letter to the Hebrews puts on the lips of Christ the following words as He comes into this world: "Sacrifices and offerings thou hast not desired, but a body thou hast prepared for me; in burnt offerings and sin offerings thou hast taken no pleasure. Then I said, 'Lo, I have come to do thy will, O God', as it is written of me in the roll of the book" (*Heb. 10:5-7*). To the disciples who brought him food at Samaria, Jesus said "My food is to do the will of him, who sent me, and to accomplish his work" (*Jn. 4:34*). And in Gethsemane he prayed, "Abba, Father, all things are possible to thee; remove this cup from me; yet not what I will, but what thou wilt" (*Mk. 14:36*). Jesus' acceptance of the Father's will, made it possible for God to carry out the work of salvation through the Passion, Death and Resurrection of Christ. When we pray that God's will may be done, we are praying that the design of God for the salvation and happiness of man may be realised.

By the phrase, 'as it is in heaven', we mean that the will of God which is already fully realised in heaven may be also equally totally realised on the earth.

### Give us this day our daily bread

The "Thou-Petitions" are over, and now we begin the "We-Petitions". The Greek word for 'daily' is *'epiousios'* and also means 'for tomorrow'. The translation should really be, "Our bread for the morrow, give us today". Tomorrow, as Joachim Jeremias says, may not only mean that next day, but also the great tomorrow, the final consummation. This petition then would have an eschatological sense and would be a request for the bread of the age of salvation, or for the bread of life. What we are praying for then, is the sustenance needed to walk faithfully in the kingdom. Some Fathers of the Church have also applied it to the Eucharist.

But this petition surely also refers to the material food, the bread needed for the nourishment of the body. The word for bread, in Hebrew *'lechem'*, and in Aramaic *'lachma'* means not so much bread as "that which is necessary for life". By bread then we mean not only the food but also clothing, shelter, and everything else needed to live in this world.

Asking us to pray for 'daily bread', Jesus also teaches us to live one day at a time, and not to worry or be anxious about the distant and unknown future: "Therefore, I tell you, do not be anxious about your life, what you shall eat or what you shall drink, nor about your body, what you shall put on. Is not life more than food, and the body more than clothing?... For the

Gentiles seek all these things; and your heavenly Father knows that you need them all. But seek first his kingdom and his righteousness, and all these things shall be yours as well" (*Mt. 6:25-26; 32-33*). Like the people of Israel in the desert who had daily portion of manna from heaven, and they were to, take only what was needed for the day (*Ex. 16:1-36*), Jesus teaches us to ask for the bread needed just for the day. Everyday we are called upon to acknowledge our need before God, living in this way in poverty of spirit which entitles us to possess the kingdom (*Mt. 5:3*).

### Forgive us our sins

Matthew has 'forgive us our debts' while Luke has 'forgive us our sins'. It is because of the two different ways of translating the original Aramaic word *'hobha'* which can mean both debt as well as sin. The expression is first of all eschatological in meaning. What is prayed for is above all for God's gracious forgiveness on the great day of reckoning that is approaching. But this petition is not only for future forgiveness. It also prays for forgiveness already today.

The age of the Messiah is essentially the age of forgiveness, and the Kingdom of God is essentially the mystery of forgiveness revealed to us in the Cross of Christ. The Good News that Christianity announces to the world is that in the Cross of Christ, God has forgiven men their sins and free pardon is offered for all who repent and accept this forgiveness. Jesus Christ during His Public life befriended tax collectors and sinners. He expressly declared that His mission was precisely this: 'The Son of Man came to seek and to save the lost" (*Lk. 19:10*) Those who are well have no need of a physician but those who are sick; I have come not to call the righteous, but sinners" (*Mk. 2:17*). A Christian needs to receive forgiveness every day because every day he falls short of the ideals of the Kingdom and commits sins.

### As we forgive those who sin against us

This does not mean that God's measure of forgiveness of our sins is according to our measure of forgiveness of others. Our imperfect forgiveness of others can never be compared with God's forgiveness which is unlimited and total. But nevertheless there is a sense in which the measure of our forgiveness affects the measure of God's forgiveness. God's forgiveness becomes effective in us in accordance with our own disposition to forgive. The phrase 'as we forgive' points to a decision to forgive others. Luke has "for we ourselves forgive every one to us". And according to Joachim Jeremias the translation of Matthew should rather be, "as we also forgive herewith our debtors".

The reason why we should forgive others is that we ourselves have been forgiven by God. This is brought

out vividly by the parable of the unmerciful servant
(*Mt. 18:23-35*). The debt the fellow servant owed him
is insignificant compared with debt he has been forgiv-
en by the king, which is enormous. Since the forgiveness we have received from God is boundless, we must
also be ready to forgive our brother seventy times seven
(*Mt. 18:22*). In Mk. 11:25 Jesus says: "Whenever you
stand praying, forgive, if you have anything against
anyone; so that your Father also who is in heaven may
forgive you your trespasses". Indeed this forgiveness is
so important that even the offering of sacrifice must be
interrupted to go and be reconciled with the brother
first (*Mt. 5:23ff*).

## Lead us not into temptation

The word *'peirasmos'* (temptation) in Greek stands for
the final persecution and testing which is to take place
before the end of the world. Failing in this temptation can
mean falling away from God irrevocably and being cut
off from Him forever. Therefore the Our Father ends in
an urgent plea and cry of anguish at this terrible prospect,
begging the Father to be preserved from it.

Joachim Jeremias, in his book, *'Unknown Sayings of
Jesus'* (London, Greenwich, 1964) speaks of the following saying of Jesus not recorded in the Gospels: 'No one
can obtain the Kingdom of heaven who has not passed
through temptation'. God Himself tempts no one (*Jam.*

*1:13*) but God allows men to be tempted and put to the test, because when they overcome the temptation it will accrue to their glory. We see in the Bible how Adam and Eve, Abraham, Moses, the people of Israel, Job, and Tobit were tempted. Jesus Christ Himself immediately after His baptism is led by the Spirit into the desert to be tempted by the devil (*Mt. 4:1-11 and parallels*). "For we have not a high priest who is unable to sympathise with our weaknesses, but one who in every respect has been tempted as we are, yet without sinning" (*Heb. 4:15*), and because of this He can help those who are tempted (*Heb. 2:18*). The Christian too will have to face temptations, but he can always be sure of the help of his Master. Jesus said to Peter, "Simon, Simon, behold Satan demanded to have you that he might sift you like wheat, but I have prayed for you that your faith may not fail; and when you have turned again, strengthen your brethren" (*Lk. 22:31-32*).

## But deliver us from evil

The word for 'Evil' is *'Ponerou'* and it can be translated as 'Evil' or 'Evil One'. While Augustine preferred 'Evil' the Greek Fathers and Tertullian and Cyprian, interpreted the word in personal sense: 'Deliver us from the Evil One, i.e. Satan'. The New Testament often speaks of Satan as the Evil One (*Mt. 13:19; Jn. 17:15; 1 Jn. 2:13, 14; 3:12; 5:18-19, Eph. 6:16*). St Peter says: "Be sober, be watchful. Your adversary the devil prowls around like a roaring lion, seeking someone to devour" (*1 Pet. 5:8*).

## Conclusion

Introducing the Our Father, Jesus says: "Pray then like this" (*Mt. 6:9*). The Our Father is the pattern of all Christian prayer, a school of prayer, the expression of our intimate relationship with the Father in Jesus Christ. A lifetime of meditation cannot exhaust the depths of this prayer. It is a prayer that can lead us to the deepest contemplation and intimacy with God.

## CALLING ON THE NAME OF THE LORD

"And it shall be that whoever calls on the name of the Lord shall be saved" (*Acts. 2:21*). Calling on the name of the Lord, the prayer of the name of Jesus, was practised from the earliest times. To understand the deep significance of this prayer we must see its meaning in the Bible and tradition of the Church.

### The Jesus prayer

The Greek Orthodox Church has preserved the tradition of the constant uninterrupted calling upon the divine name of Jesus. In the West this tradition was made known by the book, *"The Way of a Pilgrim"* which narrates the adventures of a Russian Pilgrim who travels from place to place looking for someone who can teach him to pray without ceasing. The book says that on 24th Sunday of Pentecost while in Church he heard the passage from the first letter of St Paul to the Thessalonians in which he exhorts the Christians to pray without ceasing: "Pray constantly" (*1 Thess. 5:17*). He was so impressed by these words that he does not rest until he can find someone who will show him how to fulfil this word. After nearly a year of search he meets a monk who teaches him the Jesus prayer. It consists in the constant uninterrupted calling upon the divine name of Jesus with the Heart and lips, with one's whole mind and attention, while forming a mental picture of His constant presence and imploring His grace. The prayer used is that of the blind man of Jericho slightly modified: "Lord Jesus Christ, Son of God, have pity on me" (*Mk. 10:48*). The blind man repeats this prayer again and again until Jesus stops and calls him to Him and hears his prayer. To pray the name of Jesus, is then to invoke His name uninterruptedly at work, while journeying, at leisure, on all occasions and in all needs and always. In reality this prayer sums up the whole of the Scriptures and the Gospels in particular.

### Revelation of the Name of God

The high point of the revelation of God to Moses on Sinai is the revelation of His name. When Moses asks Him for His name, God says: "I am who I am. Say this to the people of Israel, I am has sent me to you". God also said to Moses, "Say this to the people of Israel, 'The Lord, the God of your fathers, the God of Abraham, the God of Jacob, has sent me to you, this is my name forever, and thus I am to be remembered throughout all generations (*Ex. 3:14-15*). And again in Ex. 6:2-3 we read: "And God said to Moses, I am the Lord, I appeared to Abraham, to Jacob, as God Almighty, but by my name the Lord I did not make myself known to them'. (*Ex. 6:2-3*)

The name Yahweh in the Bible stands for the nature, the character and the personality of God in so far as it is known and revealed to us. Thus in Ps. 9:10 we read: "Those who know thy name put their trust in thee", and again in Ps. 20:7 "Some boast of chariots and some of horses, but we boast of the name of the Lord our God". What the psalmist means here is that, because to the people of Israel has been revealed the nature and character of God, they can put their trust in His power and saving love. When in Ex. 33 Moses prays to God to show him His glory, God tells him: "I will make all my goodness pass before you, and will proclaim before you my name: 'The Lord' And again 'The Lord passed before him and proclaimed, 'The Lord, the Lord, a God merciful and gracious, slow to anger, and abounding in steadfast love and faithfulness, keeping steadfast love for thousands, forgiving iniquity and transgression and sin, but who will by no means clear the guilty, visiting the iniquity of the fathers upon the children and the children's children, to the third and fourth generation". (*Ex. 34:6-7*)

God will give his people a place (the temple of Jerusalem) where He will make His name to dwell. In his prayer on the day of dedication Solomon calls the temple, "this house the place of which thou hast said, 'my name shall be there" (*1 Kgs. 8:29*). On that day he begged God that the people of Israel, when they are in exile because of their sins, or when they are experiencing famine or drought, or pestilence, or war or sickness and turn toward the temple and acknowledge His name and pray and make supplication to Him in this house (*1 Kgs. 8:33*), they be granted their prayer. Joel says: "And it shall come to pass the all who call upon the name of the Lord shall be delivered" (*Joel 2:32*) and Zechariah: "They will call on my name, and I will answer them. I will say, 'They are my people'; and they will say, 'The Lord is my God'". (*Zech. 13:9*)

## Revelation of the name given to Christ at the Resurrection

In the letter to Philippians St Paul says that after Jesus' self-emptying and *kenosis*, "God has highly exalted Him and bestowed on Him the name which is above every name, that at the name of Jesus every knee should bow, in heaven and on earth and under the earth, and every tongue confess that Jesus Christ is Lord, to the glory of God the Father" (*Phil. 2:9-11*). Concluding his proclamation of the Good News to the people on Pentecost day St Peter said: "Let all the house of Israel therefore know assuredly that God has made him both Lord and Christ, this Jesus whom you crucified" (*Acts. 2:36*). The apostles work miracles in the name of Jesus Christ. Peter and John heal the lame man at the gate of the temple in the name of Christ. Explaining this miracle to the crowds who had gathered, St Peter says, "And His name, by faith in His name, has made this man strong, whom you see and know" (*Acts. 3:16*).

The criterion of salvation is whether they have believed in His name: 'He who does not believe is condemned already because he has not believed in the name of the only Son of God" (*Jn. 3:18*). And again 'But to all who received him, who believed in His name, He gave power to become children of God" (*Jn. 1:12*). In Rom 10:12-13 St Paul says: "For there is no distinction between Jew and Greek; the same Lord is Lord of all and bestows his riches upon all who call upon him. For every one who calls upon the name of the Lord will be saved". Believing and calling upon the name of the Lord is the condition of salvation.

## Summary of the Gospels

This prayer in reality sums up the whole of the Gospels. The Gospels narrate how the man, Jesus of Nazareth has fulfilled the prophecies of the Old Testament and is hence the Messiah and at the same time, the Incarnate Son of God. To Him all authority in heaven and on earth is given so that He is the Lord of the living and the dead. The words "Lord Jesus Christ, Son of God" are thus in reality a deep profession of faith, expressing as they do all that we know and believe about Jesus Christ from the Scripture and from the experience and teaching of the Church.

By the words 'have mercy on me a sinner"; we put ourselves face to face with Him in an attitude of total humility, and with a contrite heart. The phrase expresses our helplessness to save ourselves or manage our lives by our own strength. This was the prayer of the Canaanite woman whose daughter was possessed by a devil (*Mt. 15:22*), of the ten lepers (*Lk. 17:13*) and of the blind men of Jericho (*Mt. 20:30*). 'This was also the prayer of the tax collector when he went to pray in the temple (*Lk. 18:13*). And in every case their prayer was heard; for the Lord cannot refuse His help to any one calling upon His name from the depth of his heart.

## The meaning of the term Mercy

In Hebrew the word for 'mercy' comes from the word *'Rahamim'* and derives from a root meaning 'womb'. It symbolises the feeling of love and compassion a mother has for her child. Thus in Is. 49:15 the Lord says: "Can a woman forget her sucking child, that she should have no compassion on the son of her womb?" The Hebrews considered the bowels as the seat of pity. It is used in the Bible only for Yahweh's relationship with his covenanted people. When Jesus was confronted with human misery and suffering, the Gospels use the word *'Splangnizomai'* which literally means "to be moved to one's bowels" (*Cf. Mt. 9:36; 14:14; 20:34; 15:32 and parallels*). This compassion which He felt always led him to act to bring succour and healing. It led Him to heal the blind (*Mt. 20:34*), to cure the leper (*Mk. 1:41*) to teach the ignorant (*Mk. 6:34*) to raise the dead (*Lk. 7:13-14*) to feed the hungry (*Mt. 15:32; Mk. 8:2*).

When we pray for mercy therefore, we are begging the Lord to show his compassion on us whom he has redeemed through His blood and made His own by Baptism. We are reminding Him of His love for us and begging Him to act in our favour, saving and healing us.

In Greek the word 'have mercy' is *'eleison'* from the word *'eleeo'* which comes from the same root as *'Elaion'* which means olive tree and the oil from it. Olive oil was used to anoint priests and kings, and is a symbol of the Holy Spirit. Kings and priests had conferred on them the spirit and the graces and the strength they needed to fulfil their duties as leaders of God's people in the spiritual and temporal spheres. When we say 'have mercy on us', we are in reality asking for the Holy Spirit.

A second use of the olive oil was as a medication for wounds. Thus we read that the good Samaritan poured oil on the wounds of the wounded man to soothe and to heal. When we pray for mercy we are therefore also praying for the healing of our wounds of sin and begging for strength and grace needed to fulfil His will.

## Conclusion

Prayer is essentially standing face to face with God. When we are in His presence, His presence should so overwhelm us as to collect and focus all our energies, thoughts, emotions and will, making us nothing but attentive. The problem with most of us in prayer is that the awareness of the presence of God is very feeble and weak. The act of faith which we make in affirming, 'God is here' often carries too little weight. We find our minds wandering and attention fading away. We find it very difficult to remain absolutely collected, and still and attentive in His presence. The early Fathers of the Church and the Orthodox tradition give us a simple way of learning to concentrate: Their method is: choose a prayer, be it Lord's Prayer or another short prayer like "Lord Jesus Christ, Son of God, have pity on me a sinner", take your stand before God, become aware of where you are and what you are doing and pronounce the words of the prayer attentively. After a certain time you will discover that your thoughts have wandered; then restart the prayer, the words, or the sentence which was the last you pronounced attentively. Pronounce the words unhurriedly, attentively, meaning what you say and go on repeating the prayer over and over again. In no time it will lead to concentration and a deep awareness of the presence of God enabling one to stand with an undivided heart, undivided will and undivided mind before the Lord. The simple prayer of the name of Jesus can lead one very soon to a deep intimacy with the indwelling Divine Guest.

## READING THE WORD

### *Lectio Divina*

"Be attentive to the reading of Scriptures" (*1 Tim. 4:13*). "And when I looked, behold a hand was stretched out to me, and a written scroll was in it; and he spread it before me; and it had writing on the front and on the back, and there were written on it words of lamentation and mourning and woe. And he said to me, 'Son of man' eat what is offered to you, eat this scroll and go speak to the house of Israel. Then I ate it; and it was in my mouth as sweet as honey" (*Ezek. 2:9; 3:1, 3*).

"Man, shall not live by bread alone, but by every Word that proceeds from the mouth of God'(*Mt. 4:4*). Listening to the Word of God is not just a luxury but a *sine-qua-non* for us to live a genuine Christian life.

### Start with prayer

Daily reading of the Bible is the first step in listening to God, speaking to us through the Scriptures. We do not read the Scriptures as one reads a novel, or a book of history or science. A novel is read for revelation, a book of history or science for information and knowledge. But the aim of reading the Scriptures is different: it is to come into contact with a living person, Jesus Christ, the Word made flesh. Hence all reading must begin with prayer, turning our hearts and minds to God to whom we want to listen. When someone begins to speak to us we turn to him and look at his face. We need to take some time before we begin to read to put ourselves in the presence of God. To listen to the Word of God speaking to us, we must first of all silence all other noises within, put away from our minds all distractions, cares and concerns and come face to face with God. Often this will take some time. The "Jesus Prayer" is the best for this. For two or three minutes, close the eyes and entering into the presence of the Lord in the heart, repeat the invocation very slowly: "Lord Jesus Christ, Son of God, have pity on me a sinner". Beg pardon for your sins. Ask the Lord to speak to you and ask him for His Spirit: "Send forth your Spirit O Lord and open my heart and mind to you".

The attitude we must bring to the reading of Scripture is that of a lover waiting at the trysting-place, longing for the moment when he can see the face of his beloved and hear her voice. "Speak, Lord, for thy servant hears" (*1 Sam. 3:9-10*). There are some Psalms which express very well this longing and this expectation. If we have time we can pray one of these Psalms slowly, making it our prayer. The following Psalms are apt for this purpose: 4, 9, 20, 27, 40, 61, 63, 86, 106, 143. In reading the Scriptures we pay attention not only to the message, but to Him who speaks it. Mary Magdalene by paying attention to the voice that called her was able to recognise the presence of the Lord and meet Jesus (*Jn. 20:16*).

### Read attentively

The Scriptures must be read slowly, carefully, prayerfully, in such a way that the meaning sinks in. We should give time to grasp the meaning not only with our heads but also with our hearts. As we read we must make pauses to reflect on what we have read and to speak to God. Speaking on the monastic tradition of *Lectio Divina*, Bouyer says, "It is a personal reading of the Word of God, during which we try to assimilate its contents; it is a reading in faith, in a spirit of prayer, being in the actual presence of God who speaks to us through the sacred text, while we try to make ourselves present to the Lord in a spirit of obedience, of total abandonment to the promises and divine demands". It is a reading done not alone, but with God.

The Fathers of the Church do not consider inspiration only as something that influenced the writers at the time of giving us the inspired texts, but as a perennial influence, always actual and operative every time they are read.

As we read we must keep in mind the form and content of the passage.

*Form:* Is the passage a parable, a miracle story, an intimate scene from the life of Jesus, a conflict story, a discourse of Jesus? Or in the Old Testament: Is it an historical narration, a prophecy, a psalm, a wisdom saying or proverb? etc.

*Content:* When we read the passage we must first try to grasp the main idea, "the fundamental assertion" of the author. This can be done by asking ourselves two questions: What does the inspired author want to tell us through this passage? What is he trying to get across? What is the point the author is trying to make? And secondly, what are the key words? Other questions that can help us to understand the message of the author are: Who are the actors in this story? How do they intersect with Jesus? With whom can you identify yourself? What are the ideas expressed in this text? How smoothly or abruptly do they progress? What are the different sections in this text? How can they be divided? What is the context in which this passage occurs?

God's Word must be read slowly and savoured. While we need to understand the broad sweep of the passage, we must also be attentive to the details and nuances.

### A continual reading

Reading a short passage at random is useful but not enough. Holy Scripture does not consist of individual passages, it is a unit and is intended to be read as such. As George Martin says in his book, *'Reading Scripture as the Word of God'*, "It is only in the infiniteness of its inner relationships, in the connection of the Old and New Testaments, of promise and fulfilment, sacrifice and worship, law and the Gospel, cross and Resurrection, faith and obedience that the full significance of the scriptures are perceived". But starting from the book of Genesis and reading through the Bible up to the last verse of the last chapter of the Book of Revelation is not advisable. First of all, the books in the Bible are not found in the order in which they were written, nor even in the historical order of the events they describe. Since we read as Christians it is better to start with the New Testament, and in the New Testament with the Gospels of Mark, Matthew, Luke and Acts, followed by the letters of Paul beginning with the letters to the Thessalonians, and going on to Corinthians, Romans, Galatians and the rest of the Pauline and non-Pauline epistles. John's Gospel and the three Johannine letters could then be read. They require very attentive reading as they contain deep insights of the mystery of Christ and of our relationship with Him as His disciples; a lot of prayerful attention and thought is needed to grasp their full meaning. The Apocalypse is the most difficult book of the New Testament and it is important to consult a good commentary while reading it.

Coming to the Old Testament, the Book of Exodus (not Genesis) must be read first to be followed by the book of Genesis and the other books of the Pentateuch. Before reading the books of the Prophets, the historical books of the Old Testament from Joshua to second book of Kings must be read, because they provide the background for the prophets. In the prophetical literature it is better to start with Amos, followed by Hosea, Micah, Zephaniah, Isaiah, Jeremiah, Ezekiel and the others. After this the rest of the books of the Old Testament can be read.

### Faith, faithfulness and humility

Faith is the first requisite for encountering Christ in the Scriptures. We spoke of this earlier. Only through the eyes of faith can we see the face of Christ in the Scriptures and hear Him speaking to us through them: "Did not our hearts burn within us while he talked to us on the road, while He opened to us the Scriptures"? (*Lk. 24:32*). If we are faithful to our daily reading of Scriptures we will experience that our reading fills us with deep joy and peace and make our hearts burn with love. But there will be also days when the Scriptures may seem dull and uninspiring. If we do not relax our efforts, in due time we shall reap our harvest. We need humility to accept the fact the Word of God is much bigger than us and that often we do not understand everything. As we enter more fully into the mystery of Christ, they will become more meaningful for us. We should never give up our reading. We need to fix a time that is most appropriate for us during the day and be faithful to it. The amount of time we can devote to the reading of Scripture will vary from person to person. A fifteen minutes schedule, morning and evening would be a good proposition.

## MEDITATING THE WORD

### *Meditatio*

"And these words which I command you this day shall be upon your heart; and you shall teach them diligently to your children, and shall talk of them when you sit in your house, and when you walk by the way, and when you lie down, and when you rise. And you shall bind them as a sign upon your hand and they shall be as frontlets between your eyes. And you shall write them on the door posts of your house and on your gates' (*Deut. 6:6-9*).

In the parable of the sower, Jesus Christ compares the Word to a seed. The seed is the Word of God (*Lk. 8:1 1*). A seed is a very wonderful thing. It looks lifeless, a dead thing, almost like a stone. But it is not a dead thing but something living and alive. It enfolds in itself immense potentialities and powers. Just place it in good moist soil, and at once its magic powers are released; it springs to life, sprouts forth, sends out leaves and roots and becomes a plant, yielding blossoms and fruits that can nourish and sustain the life of people. Jesus Christ says that the Word of God is like this. It too has immense potentialities and powers. But to be effective it must fall into a warm receptive heart, where the kernel of the Word can be broken open and its life-giving powers released.

"Unless a grain of wheat fails into the earth and dies, it remains alone; but if it dies, it bears much fruit" (*Jn. 12:24*). "As the rain and the snow come down from heaven, and return not thither but water the earth, making it bring forth and sprout, giving seed to the sower and bread to the eater, so shall my word be that goes forth from my mouth; it shall not return to me empty, but it shall accomplish that which I purpose, and prosper in the thing for which I sent it" (*Is. 55: 10-11*).

Meditation is the process by which this is realised. The Bible defines meditation as murmuring with the lips. (*Ps. 1:2*). It is repeating quietly the passage over and over, putting questions to the text until it is assimilated and interiorized. The Fathers of the Church use the image of chewing the cud. To assimilate what was eaten, the cow quietly settles down and masticates what was consumed. In the same way the text read must be reflected upon, savoured and absorbed. Even the shortest verse in the Bible, "Jesus wept" (*Jn. 11:35*) has depths of meaning. There are many verses in Scripture whose meaning we will not exhaust, in a lifetime of reflection and meditation. A Father of the Church defines meditation thus: "To mediate is to read and reread, to masticate and mutter, to ruminate and recite, to fix the word in mind and to preserve it in the heart, not for the sake of disputation or even to arouse good sentiments but for prayer, for contemplation and hence for action". Meditation is the rumination and mastication of the Word.

It is to "taste and see that the Lord is good" (*Ps. 34:8*). It is going over the text read in mind, to discover its central theme, recalling the key words again and again imprinting them in the heart, so as to be able to draw from the text, like a scribe, things old and new (*Mt. 13:52*). Through meditation the sacred text becomes the life giving Word of God. If the Scriptures are like a well, it is through meditation that we draw the living waters from it.

### Read the Word in a situation of 'today'

To achieve this, first of all we must learn to read the Word of God in a situation of 'Today', as words spoken to us personally by God, as a personal communication from the Father to us. The Word we read, it is true, is bound to an event in the past, to a history that is different from ours, but being a force and power of God, it recreates for us a new 'today' every time we hear it. "O that today you would listen to his voice" (*Ps. 95:8*). Jesus Christ after reading the passage from Isaiah in the synagogue of Nazareth says: "Today this Scripture has been fulfilled in your hearing' (*Lk. 4:21*). When we read the Words of Christ in the Gospel we should listen to them as though they were spoken to us personally by Christ. When we read a letter of St Paul, we should read it as though it was a letter written to us personally.

It is thus that St Paul and the New Testament authors use the Scriptures. Thus applying the incidents in the Old

Testament to the life of the Corinthians, St Paul says: "I want you to know brethren that, our fathers were all under the cloud and all passed through the sea;... Nevertheless with most of them God was not pleased for they were overthrown in the wilderness. Now these things are warnings for us not to desire evil as they did". (*1 Cor. 10:6*) And again in the letter to the Romans: "For whatever was written in former days was written for our instruction, that by steadfastness and by the encouragement of the Scriptures we might have hope" (*Rom. 15:4*). Again in Corinthians, we see how he quotes from the Old Testament and applies directly to his readers: "for it is written in the law of Moses, 'You shall not muzzle an ox when it is treading out the grain' Is it for oxen that God is concerned? Does he not speak entirely for our sake? It was written for our sake, because the ploughman should plough in hope and the thresher in hope of a share in the crop. If we have sown spiritual good among you, is it too much if we reap your material benefits?" (*1 Cor. 9:9-11*).

Again in the letter to the Romans, discussing Abraham's faith, he says: "But the words, 'it was reckoned to him' were written not for his sake alone, but for ours also. It will be reckoned to us who believe in him that raised from the dead Jesus Our Lord, who was put to death for our trespasses and raised for our justification"

Thus when we read the Words God spoke to the people of Israel through Jeremiah: "I have loved you with an everlasting love; therefore I have continued my faithfulness to you" (*Jer. 31:3*), we will hear them as spoken to us assuring us of His unfailing love for us personally. Or when in the Gospel Jesus says, "No one can serve two masters; for either he will hate the one and love the other, or he will be devoted to the one and despise the other. You cannot serve God and mammon' (*Mt. 6:24*), we will listen to them as Words of Christ warning us that unless we give Him first place in our life, loving Him above all persons and possessions we cannot be his disciples.

"You are the man" (*2 Sam 12:5-7*) the prophet Nathan said to David after narrating the story about the rich man with very many flocks and herds who yet took the poor man's lamb to prepare a feast for his guest. After reading the Words of Scripture we too must say to ourselves: "I am the man". It is to me that these words are said. What is written is speaking about me.

## Putting questions to the text

Listening to the Word in a situation of 'Today' is only the first step. The second is to assimilate and interiorise it, trying to savour it and capture the depth of its significance for us personally. This can be done by putting questions to the text:

- What is the point the author is trying to make?
- What does it mean for me today?
- What is Christ telling me personally through this

text, about Himself, about my relationship to Him,
to others?

• How does this passage illuminate the concrete
problem I am facing in my life: work, sins, sickness,
sufferings, misunderstandings, family life,
relationship with others etc?

It is very important also to be alert to the broad context of
the entire Bible, because the Bible explains itself. See if
you can recall any other passage that speaks about the
same thing or can illuminate this passage.

It will be of great help trying to relive the whole scene,
trying to visualise what the author is saying as vividly as
possible, with our mental eye. We must sit at the feet of
Jesus as first century disciples in order to listen to the
Word speaking to us in the twenty first century.

### The action of the spirit within us

The rest is the Spirit's work in us. On our part we can listen, reflect, pray, but it is for the Lord to do the speaking,
to give understanding to our minds and touch our hearts.
St Paul says: "Likewise the Spirit helps us in our weakness; for we do not know how to pray as we ought, but
the Spirit himself intercedes for us with sighs too deep for
words. And he who searches the hearts of men knows
what is the mind of the Spirit, because the Spirit intercedes for the saints according to the will of God'. (*Rom.
8:26-27*). The Spirit has been given to us by the Father

precisely for this. We must never forget that this Spirit really dwells in us and in accordance with the level of our faith, He will really act in us and pray in us. Jesus promised us this when He said: "These things I have spoken to you while still with you. But the Counsellor, the Holy Spirit, whom the Father will send in my name, He will teach you all things and bring to your remembrance all that I have said to you" (*Jn. 14:25-28*). It is through the work of the Spirit alone that the words of Scripture can become living Words for us and that through them we are able to enter into communion with God who thus reveals Himself to us.

Bengel said: *"Te totum applica ad textum, rem totam applica ad te"*. (Apply yourself wholly to the text and apply its matter wholly to yourself). God, when He inspired the Scriptures thousands of years ago, had us also in mind, and today when we read them again, He is always present to address Himself to us through them. Two things therefore are important for meditation: first, act of faith in the actual presence of this God who speaks to us today through the Scriptures and secondly our personal self-adherence, faith, abandonment and self-donation to Him who speaks to us. If in this way we meditate and assimilate the Scriptures, they will begin to speak to us and the current of the Spirit that inspired them will flow freely into our lives and transform us.

## PRAYING THE WORD

### *Oratio*

"And in praying do not heap up empty phrases as the gentiles do; for they think that they will be heard for their many words. Do not be like them, for your Father knows what you need before you ask him" (*Mt. 6:7-8*).

### Prayer is the response caused in us by God's Word

Our prayers can become empty phrases without content; some formulas learnt by heart in childhood! Jesus Christ calls this type of prayer "pagan" (*Mt. 6:7*). In this type of prayer the initiative comes from man, who tries to inform the deity, and by some gifts or other ways persuade the god to hear and grant his request. Jesus Christ says that Christian prayer is radically different from this and tells us that, "the Father already knows what you need before you ask him" (*Mt. 6:8*). Christian prayer starts from the initiative of God. It is God who through the Word, through His action, and His Grace in us, moves us to pray. Christian prayer is the response to God's Word. The Word of God we have heard or read attentively and interiorized through meditation moves us to prayer.

### It is the action of the spirit within us

It is the Spirit in us that moves us to prayer. The Word has been realised, fulfilled, become flesh in us and is given back to God as we respond to Him. St Paul says: "Because you are sons, God has sent the Spirit of His Son into our hearts, crying, "Abba! Father!" (*Gal. 4:6*). This is the summary of all Christian prayer: to address the Father: "Abba! Father!". Prayer is to speak to the Father.

### Prayer is loving

St Theresa defined prayer as a heart to heart conversation with Him who loves us, and insisted that prayer does not consist in thinking much, but loving much. Prayer is loving. It is an encounter between two lovers, God and the Christian. God speaks to the Christian revealing His love for him. The Word of God comes to stir his heart to sentiments of love and gratitude, thanksgiving and praise and at the same time sentiments of deep contrition and sorrow at his own unfaithfulness, sinfulness and blindness. In the early Church prayer was rarely intercession, but was essentially a word sung, proclaimed, said again, recalled and meditated upon. Prayer in the Scripture is first of all praise and thanksgiving. St Theophan, the Russian recluse of the 18th Century wrote: "Prayer is turning the mind and thoughts towards God. To pray means to stand before God with mind in the heart, for in this lies the essence of the matter".

Standing face to face with God who loves you and is speaking to you and responding to Him. This is prayer. The actual form of prayer will vary according to the intensity of the love each one has for the Lord. As our love for the Lord grows, so also will our prayer vary and grow in depth and intensity.

## Praying the story of the blind man of Jericho

If for instance we read the story of the cure of the blind man of Jericho (*Mk. 10:46-52*) and having meditated on it, we want to make it the subject matter of our prayer: the first thing the Word does through reading attentively and meditating would be, like the blind man, to make us come face to face with Jesus Christ, because in reality we are that blind man. We too are blind spirituality. In our meditation, the Lord will have convinced us of our inner blindness and hardness of heart. This in turn will make us cry out like the blind man: "Jesus Son of David have mercy on me!" (*Mk. 10:47*). The text says the blind man cried not once or twice, but many times. He was desperate because he knew that it was his only chance. And he does not even pay attention to the rebukes of the others, so intensely was he aware of the darkness, of the continual night in which he lived. When the Word has illumined us laying bare the depth of our own darkness and sinfulness, we too will break forth into prayer. For the blind man the moment Jesus called him and asked him, "What do you

want me to do for you?" (*Mk. 10:51*) was a moment of
deep personal communion with the Master. There prayer
also takes on a deeper and more personal dimension.
"Master let me receive my sight' and he hears from Him
the words: "Go your way; your faith has made you well"
(*Mt. 10:52*). The darkness gives way to the marvel of
broad daylight. For the first time he looked at the face of
the Master, of other people. For the first time he saw the
sun, the trees, the flowers. Then probably overwhelmed
with joy he fell at the master's feet and thanked him pro-
fusely and recounted to others the marvellous cure He
had done for him and praised Him. When in prayer we
meet the Lord face to face and an intense communion of
hearts takes place filling our hearts with love and joy, we
naturally break forth into adoration, praise and thanksgiving. The Gospel says of the blind man: 'And immediately
he received his sight and followed him on the way" (*Mt.
10:52*). Our encounter with God in prayer will necessarily
flow into our life which becomes a more intense and
more faithful following of Christ.

## The Word judges and saves

The Word of God has a two fold action. It is a two-edged
sword: "for the Word of God is living and active, sharper
than any two-edged sword, piercing to the division of
soul and spirit, of joints and marrow, and discerning the
thoughts and intentions of the heart" (*Heb. 4:11-12*). The

Word first of all enlightens us, showing us who we really are, what in truth there is in our heart, our true attitudes, thoughts and intentions which often are contrary to the Gospel. But as the Word enlightens, it also heals and saves: enlightening and judging, healing and saving. We will come away from prayer always a little more aware of our sinfulness, but a little more aware also of God's great love for us who forgives us and accepts us as we are and gives us the grace to walk in newness of life.

A loving colloquy is not made only of exchange of words but also of silences which can be eloquent because they speak to God about our emptiness in front of His fullness; or it can be just being in His presence, being inflamed by His Spirit within us, contemplating His face or resting in His loving care, like Mary sitting at the feet of Jesus in silence. But here prayer has become contemplation of which we speak in the next chapter.

## CONTEMPLATING THE WORD

### *Contemplatio*

"Now when the angels had gone from them into heaven, the shepherds said to one another, 'Let us go to Bethlehem and see this thing that has happened which the Lord has made known to us'. So they hurried away and found Mary and Joseph, and the baby lying in the manger. When they saw the child they repeated what they had been told about him, and everyone who heard it was astonished at what the shepherds had to say. As for Mary, she treasured all these things and pondered them in her heart" (*Lk. 2:15-20*).

### Mary the contemplative

In the second chapter of his Gospel, Luke presents to us Mary as the one who is continually contemplating the events of Jesus' life. After the shepherds returned, the evangelist says, "Mary kept all these things pondering them in her heart". (*Lk. 2:19*) Again, after the loss and finding of Jesus in the temple: "And they did not understand the saying which he spoke to them... and his mother kept all these things in her heart". (*Lk. 2:50*) Surely she did not understand many things that were happening to her.

But she knew that the Lord was at work, carrying out His design of salvation for man, and she gave her total response in love at every moment: "Behold I am the handmaid of the Lord, let it be to me according to your word" (*Lk. 1:38*).

We find that Mary was present at the key moments of this work of redemption: It was at her *'fiat'* that the Word becomes flesh and the process of redemption begins. Of the thirty years of hidden life of Jesus, we have only one incident: the loss and finding of Jesus in the temple; but the narration ends with the words: "And he went down with them and came to Nazareth, and was obedient to them; and his mother kept all these things in her heart. And Jesus increased in wisdom and in stature, and in favour with God and man" (*Lk. 2:51-52*). These thirty years of the hidden life when Jesus lived under her subjection and in obedience to her must have really been years of contemplation for her: watching this baby grow and become an adult and prepare Himself for His mission. Then we find her present at the wedding feast at Cana, when Jesus inaugurates his public life by performing the first sign according to John's Gospel. This was done at her request. She was present at the foot of the cross. She was present when the Holy Spirit came down upon the apostles at Pentecost and the Church is born. But hers was always a humble and unobtrusive presence. She was not called to work any miracles or go to proclaim the Gospel publicly like the apostles. Hers was a life of contemplation and intense prayer; Mary is our model in the contemplation of the Scriptures. We too are called not merely to read, meditate and pray the Word but also contemplate the Word. The Gospel says, "Mary kept all these things" i.e., the events of Christ's birth and life, which we have in the Scriptures.

## The true reason for her greatness

Jesus says that in this consisted her greatness "Now as he was speaking, a woman in the crowd raised her voice and said, 'Blessed is the womb that bore you, and the breasts that you sucked'. But he said, 'Blessed rather are those who bear the word of God and keep it" (*Lk. 11:27-28*). In His reply Jesus does not deny that His mother was blessed. Already long before this woman, Elizabeth had proclaimed her blessed and that too moved by the Holy Spirit. And Mary herself had declared that all generations would call her blessed. Jesus therefore does not deny that His mother was indeed blessed. He only rectified her answer a little. The woman had said Mary was great because of her physical motherhood of the Messiah: 'Blessed is the womb that bore you, and the breasts that you sucked" (*Lk. 11:27*). But he said, "Blessed rather are those who hear the word of God and kept it" (*Lk. 11:28*). The real reason for Mary's greatness Jesus says, that she listened to God's Word, and kept it, that is she opened

herself completely to God's Word, to God's action in her
to such an extent that this Word was really fulfilled in her
and became flesh in her.

### Every Christian is called to be a contemplative

In this she is the type of the Church, which according to
Jesus is the community of those who listen to the Word
of God and keep it. When Jesus was told: "Your mother
and your brethren are standing outside desiring to see
you", But He said to them 'My mother and my brethren
are those who hear the Word of God and do it" (*Lk.
8:20-21*). Like Mary, Christians are those who keep the
Word of God in their hearts. And when like her they
keep the Word in their hearts it is realised and fulfilled in
them too as in Mary. "If a man loves me, he will keep
my word, and my Father will love him, and we will
come to him and make our home with him" (*Jn. 14:23*).
Indeed Jesus presents it as the condition for all genuine
discipleship: 'If you make my word, your home you will
indeed be my disciples, you will learn the truth and the
truth will make you free" (*Jn. 8:31-32*). Not only does
the Word dwell in us, but we too are called to make our
home in the Word. We are called upon to live in the
Word of Jesus as we would in a home. 'The image here
is of living in the Word of Jesus: a familiar place of
security that we can always return to, a place where we
love and are loved, a place that provides roots in a world

that sometimes perplexes us or wearies us. The image of God's Word as our home carries with it notions of intimacy and familiarity; it carries the notion that the Word of God is our primary place of rootedness in a world of change, a world that is passing away". *(George Martin, Reading Scripture as the Word of God, Michigan, 1982)*

## Through contemplation the mystery is realised in us

We are called upon to contemplate the words and events of Jesus' life and to keep them in our heart and even to make them our home. In doing this we are not merely remembering these things. Mary was not merely remembering these events but her own life was caught up by these events and she was part of them. Like her we too are called upon relive and experience these mysteries. As Fr. David M. Stanley explains beautifully, (*"Contemplation of the Gospel: Ignatius of Loyola and the Contemporary Christian", Theological Studies. 1968.*) these mysteries are not merely events of past history. The saving mysteries of the incarnation, birth, childhood and public life of Jesus' earthly history from cradle to the grave because they are deeds of the eternal Word of God, transcend the limitations of time and space and have been endowed mysteriously in His glorified humanity with a totally new and enduring actuality. In Him there is neither before nor after, but the continual now of eternity. When in the liturgy, the Church celebrates these mysteries, she is not merely recalling them, but these mysteries are actually made present through the sacramental rites of the liturgy. The Risen Lord is someone who is alive and present. He is not a figure of the past, but our contemporary. He is really present to us today and we can really encounter Him and experience His mysteries and contemplate them as Mary His mother did.

Jesus Christ through His exaltation to the Father's right hand has become the *Kyrios*, the Lord of history and nature, of persons and events. His Resurrection has not removed Him from us, but only enables Him to be more dynamically present in the world than He ever was when He walked the hills of Galilee. *'Iesous Kyrios'* Jesus is Lord, is the most primitive proclamation of faith. This awareness that the Risen Lord was alive and present in their midst is the reason why in the Gospels we do not find any nostalgia for "the good old days". There is no attempt to live in the past. The Risen Lord is present in the Church and through the Word and the Sacraments, today we can meet Him.

### The events of Christ's life have a perennial actuality

The Apocalypse presents Christ to us. I saw a Lamb "standing as though it had been slain" (*Rev. 5:6*) i.e., as the crucified and Risen Lord. When the Risen Lord appeared to the Apostles he showed them His hands and His side (*Jn. 20:20*) and He invited the doubting apostle

Thomas to put his finger in the wounds in His hands and on His side (*Jn. 20:27*). Even in His glory Jesus wears the marks of his sacred passion, thus showing that they have an enduring reality in Him. Not only His Passion and Resurrection, but also the other saving mysteries of the incarnation, birth, childhood, and public life as well as His temptations, triumphs, frustrations and disillusionments have a perennial actuality in Him who is the Lord of history and in whom the past, present and future merge into the eternal now.

Fr. Stanley brings out this truth vividly by comparing the life and works of Socrates with that of Jesus Christ: "Socrates is dead and the example of his life, however noble is in large measure a matter of past history, and since he has not yet risen as Christ did, Socrates' past (i.e., the set of human experiences which constituted it) has not gone forward into the new life with God as has the sacred humanity of Jesus Christ".

Secondly, the life and teachings of Socrates which his pupil Plato gives us are not inspired and hence: "They lack the unique quality which makes our Gospels a privileged locus of the special presence of the Spirit of the Risen Christ. Consequently, Socrates' past survives in a manner very different from that of the exalted Lord Jesus'.

And Fr. Stanley concludes: "That is to say, Jesus has not simply returned to this life. He has gone forward to a totally new life with God His Father and this in the entirety of His human nature with the whole gamut of His historical experiences. Thus all the mysteries of His life upon earth have been given a new reality in Him who has become Master of history and therefore the contemplation of the Gospel scene is no mere exercise in imagination, no mere effort at reconstruction or recall (as with the modern historian) of events whose reality lies solely in the past. The events of Jesus life, His words and teachings, are endowed perpetually with a contemporaneity or actuality in the Risen Christ such as the experience of no other human being (with the exception of Our Lady) are known to possess".

And hence though Jesus exists now, only as the exalted Lord, we can today relate to Him in His earthly mysteries of the Incarnation, Birth, Infancy, Hidden Life, Public Life, Temptations and Suffering because these experiences retain their actuality in Him as He now exists.

Indeed the sacraments and liturgy draw us into these mysteries of Christ and they are realised and actualised in us. Thus in the sacraments of Baptism and Eucharist, we die with Christ and rise with Him and receive His own Spirit, the Spirit He gave to His Apostles on the day of Pentecost. In the Sacrament of Penance the forgiveness He won on the cross is applied to us, and in the anointing of the sick, our sufferings are given a redeeming power, and they become a sharing in Christ's own passion.

## Process inverse to the formation of the Gospels

The whole Process is analogous to the formation of the Gospels. In contemplation there are the very same three-fold process as at the formation of the Gospel but in the inverse order. In the formation of the Gospel there is first the events of Christ's Incarnation, Life, Passion, Death and Resurrection. Secondly we have the period of the early Church where these events are proclaimed, reflected upon and contemplated. Finally they are written down. In contemplation of the Scriptures we start with the written Word and through a process of reflection meditation and contemplation arrive at the experience when the mystery is realised, fulfilled and so to say takes place in us, because the Spirit of Christ fulfils it in us.

That this is in accordance with the tradition of the Scriptures themselves is seen from Deut. 5:2-3 where the author described the event character of the ritual procla-mation to his own contemporaries many centuries after the covenant at Sinai: "The Lord our God made a covenant with us in Horeb. Not with our fathers did the Lord make this covenant, but with us who are all of us here alive this day". Many saints and mystics in the his-tory of the Church especially the stigmatised have had this experience even in a physical way. They bore the marks of Christ's Passion in their body and relived not only His Passion, but His whole life and events of His life from cradle to the grave. What they were given to experience physically we are called to experience in faith, through the contemplation of the Gospels.

## Conclusion

Jesus says in the Sermon on the Mount: "When you pray, go in to your room and shut the door, and pray to your Father who is in secret; and your Father who sees in secret will reward you (*Mt. 6:6*). Whereas in reading, meditation and prayer the spiritual faculties of intellect, memory and will are very active, in contemplation on the other hand, God shuts the door of our faculties to particular images and concepts and communes directly and immediately with the soul. St John of the Cross says, 'At this stage our faculties are at rest. They work not actively but passively by receiving what God is effecting in them". (*St John of the Cross, The Dark Night of Soul*) And again, "Contemplation is none other than a secret, peaceful and loving infusion of God which, if the soul allows it to happen inflames it in the Spirit of love". Instead of putting questions to the text and trying to grasp the significance of the passage for us, at this stage we are led to remain still before the Lord, beholding His face and being inflamed by His love, leading to the transferring union. But this is entirely God's action in us and all we can do is to accept it gratefully when He chooses to grant it to us.

## HOW TO STUDY THE SCRIPTURES ON YOUR OWN

'All Scripture is inspired by God and profitable for teaching, for reproof, for correction, and for training in righteousness, that the man of God may be complete, equipped for every good work" (*2 Tim. 3:16-17*).

### The importance of studying the Scriptures

To be able to listen to God's Word, to understand it, and to enter into dialogue with God through prayer, meditation and contemplation, there is need of a serious effort to study the scriptures. Though considerable portions of Scriptures are clear enough, large sections of the Bible are not easy because God when speaking to man used the culture, history, language and mentality of the people of Israel, which is different from our own. We need to understand the Semitic mode of thought and expression. Besides, the books of the Bible have undergone a long process of editing before reaching the final stage. And some books of the Bible are quite complex and difficult.

Often the experience of a Christian is that of the eunuch of the Queen of Ethiopia who when Philip asked him, 'Do you understand what you are reading?" And he said, "How can I, unless someone guides me?" (*Acts*

*8:30-31*). We need to seek the help and guidance of those who are competent. The Bible is the book of the Church and we need to be guided by her. The warning in the second letter of Peter is always relevant: "First of all you must understand this, that no prophecy of scripture is a matter of one's own interpretation, because no prophecy ever came by the impulse of man, but men moved by the Holy Spirit spoke from God" (*2 Pt. 1:20-21*).

This guidance can be realised by personally attending a Bible class, where a competent teacher guides you or it can also be done making use of aids, introductions and commentaries which are reliable.

## Familiarity with the Bible is essential

But most often consulting too many commentaries only makes the study of the Bible very tedious and boring. In reality the Bible explains itself, and familiarity with the entire Bible is of prime importance. Here I propose a method of beginning the study of the Scriptures by oneself personally using just two books: The Jerusalem Bible and a good Concordance. The Jerusalem Bible has good introductions to each book, footnotes and cross references. The Concordance takes you to the other passages in the Bible where the same topic is dealt with, developed or clarified. Once this personal study has been done we can consult with profit some good commentaries.

## Study prayerfully

The study of the Scriptures must be done prayerfully and with reverence. It is not so much a question of knowing lots of things about the Bible intellectually, as that of meeting the God who revealed Himself through them. Hence the study of the Scriptures must always begin with a prayer and prayer should accompany the study. Study the Word attentively, dialoguing with God, stopping to reflect, to adore, and to praise.

The following different approaches are helpful as a practical way of studying the Scriptures. (*Tim La Haye, How to study the Bible for Yourself, California, 1976*)

## Study the Bible by books

It is good to start with some books that are not difficult and which are at the same time short: like the Letter of James, 1 John, 1 Thessalonians, etc. and then move on to the more difficult and bigger books. The first thing to do when studying a book is to try to master its contents, and this is done by reading the book over and over again a number of times. As you read try to keep the following questions in mind:

- What is the main theme and purpose of the book?
- What are the major topics dealt with by the author?
- When and why was this book written: for whom was it written? By whom was it written?
- What are the major problems discussed?

What solutions are given?
- What are the key verses?
- What does the text mean for me today?

Once you have answered these questions write down the answer to these questions in a note book, and finally write the content of the book in your own words. Once this is over consult a good commentary on the book and complete your answers.

### Study the Bible by chapters and short passages

Since the average chapters are not more than twenty-five verses, it is easier to analyse a chapter than the entire book. Each chapter has usually only one central theme. But the division of Bible into chapters and verses came only much later. The Bible was divided into chapters by Cardinal Hugo de Santo Caro about 1250 and Robert Hugo Stephens, a French printer introduced the verse divisions into the Greek New Testament. The first entire English Bible to carry both chapters and verse numbers was the Geneva Bible published in 1560. Sometimes these divisions are content-wise not exact. This must be kept in mind while analysing the chapter.

The first step again is to master the content of the chapter, by reading the chapter over and over again. As you read keep the following questions in mind:
- What is the main subject of this chapter? What is its central lesson? What are the key paragraphs?

- Who are the main people appearing in this chapter and how do they interact with each other?
- What does it say about Christ?

About our relationship with Him?

- What does it mean for me today?

One easy way to grasp the content of the chapter is to underline the verbs. This will enable you to see the flow of the passage as well as the main themes in it.

Next, write down a summary of the chapter in your own words.

Finally, analyse the key verses and words. Using a Biblical Dictionary, trace the meaning of the word in the original and then using a Concordance study its use in the entire Bible, as they are used in the various contexts. Consult a commentary to complete your understanding. The same method can be used to study the shorter passages.

### Study the Bible by themes

There are excellent books that have already done this work like: *'Dictionary of Biblical Theology'* edited by Leon Dufour, *'Encyclopedia of Biblical Theology'* edited by Bauer etc. Do not consult them first. Rather make your own personal study first. If for instance, you want to study the theme of faith in the Bible, with the help of a Concordance examine every reference to faith in the Bible from Genesis to Apocalypse, and write down in a note book. Then read through every reference taking note of the context and the various shades of meaning. Once this is done classify and group them together until they fall into basic patterns and divisions. Now consult one of the above mentioned works to complete your understanding.

## Study the Bible according to the persons

It has been calculated that there are some 2930 different men and women in the Old and New Testaments. Some are very insignificant people and are referred to only once or twice. But others are key figures like Adam, Abraham, Moses, David, Joshua, Samuel, Solomon, Peter, John, Paul, Barnabas etc. They were people through whom God carried out the work of man's salvation, and they are always examples for us. Secondly each of them in one way or another prefigures Jesus Christ or bears witness to Him. With the help of a Concordance read every passage where the name occurs, and try to grasp the relevance for us today, and how they prefigure or bear witness to Christ.

## Searching the Scriptures

Jesus told the Pharisees: "You search the Scriptures, because you think that in them you have eternal life; and it is they that bear witness to me; Yet you refuse to come to me that you may have life" (*Jn. 5:39*). The Rabbis used to practice this method. But for this we need to have a Bible with cross references and footnotes. The Jerusalem

Bible is excellent for this. Take a key verse of the Bible, preferably in the New Testament, for instance the word of Jesus in the Sermon on the Mount: "You are the salt of the earth" (*Mt. 5.13*). What did Jesus Christ mean by this? In the side there are five references, in Jerusalem Bible. The first is Mk. 9:50. Read Mk. 9:50 taking care to read the whole paragraph this verse comes in, in this way to see also the context. But Mk. 9:50 has five other side references, the first being Leviticus 2:13. Turning to Lev. 2:13 we find two other side references as well as a foot note. Read these and go on to the next side reference and so on. In this way go on searching the Scriptures, stopping often to pray and to dialogue with God. After some time stop this line and come back to the original verse in Mt. 5:13 and read the next side reference, and go on as before searching the Scriptures, and when this line is exhausted take the 3rd, 4th and 5th side references and go on in this way immersing yourself in the Scriptures. But it is important always to read prayerfully and attentively, waiting for the Lord to speak, and taking note of the insights received. Finally end with a prayer. This method is very good for Retreats and Days of Recollection when we have a lot of time at our disposal. But it can also be done on other days, devoting to the scrutiny of the Scriptures only the amount of time you are able. Write down your insights.

## Study the psalms of the Bible

There are 150 Psalms in the Bible and each one of them can be for us a source of Spiritual nourishment and prayer. Begin by reading the Psalm over and over, trying to grasp the content, the parallelism, imagery etc. Very often we come across the phenomenon known as parallelism, i.e. the second line of a Psalm repeating exactly what was said in the first in a different way or with slight modification, or addition etc.

Thus Ps. 5 says in verse 1: "Give ear to my words O Lord Give heed to my groaning." And Ps. 6 says in verse 1: "O Lord rebuke me not in thy anger, Nor chasten me in thy wrath.'

As you read the Psalm ask yourself the following questions:

- To whom is the Psalm addressed?
- What is the central theme of this Psalm?
- What are the promises, Blessings, Commandments found in this Psalm?
- Is there anything in this Psalm that pre-announces the mystery of Christ?
- What does this Psalm mean for you?

Write down your insights. Consult a good commentary to complete your findings.